ALL RILED UP

Other Books by Ted L. Carroll

The Weathering of Strawberry Ben – A Novel

The Strawberry Ben Spiritual Workbook: Co-Creating Everyday Eternal Living – An Interactive Guide for Personal Spiritual Development

Illegal Jesus: Young Male Hispanic Immigrants in Strata Fractured America – An Invitation to Americans from Within, A Social Conscience Essay

www.tedcarrollauthor@wix.com/buythebook

ALL RILED UP

A STORY OF WRECKAGE, RESTORATION, AND REBIRTH

J. RILEY HIGGINBOTHAM
& TED L. CARROLL

ARPress
ILLUMINATING IDEAS
EMPOWERING VOICES

Edited by
As You Are Publishing's Editorial Department &
The Western Consortium Writing Lab

ARPress
45 Dan Road Suite 5
Canton MA 02021

Hotline: 1(888) 821-0229
Fax: 1(508) 545-7580

Ordering Information:
Quantity sales. Special discounts are available on quantity purchases by corporations, associations, and others. For details, contact the publisher at the address above.

Printed in the United States of America.

ISBN-13:	Paperback	979-8-89389-687-9
	eBook	979-8-89389-688-6

Library of Congress Control Number: 2024923810

CONTENTS

ACKNOWLEDGEMENTS

We consider ourselves gratefully fortunate to have been brought together in such a way as to unite our spirits and talents in, quite literally, a co-creative expression.

Thank you to our families, friends, investors, helpers, and supporters of myriad kinds, who "have our backs" no matter what life brings. Our special prayers of gratitude extend to those who preordered this book, and for all current and future purchasers. Your readership means the world to us and for our future pursuits.

Thank you!

Sincerely,

Riley & Ted

PREFACE

I have known Riley since 1996. When I met him, he was a young man intent on being true to himself through means of artistic expression. Through multi-media art instruction and ceramics class, Riley and I created some cool pieces. However, Riley found his outlet, through the years, in music – and in having fun. Having fun included, besides band practice and performance, fishing, camping, partying, and working on cars.

Riley's unlikely survival from a near-fatal car wreck (December 2012) and his continued rehabilitation is nothing short of miraculous. Certainly, Riley's strong spirit as well as the love of his son, his amazing family, and supportive friends, have pulled him through the past few years into a new place – this time, the renewal of Riley's creativity and a willingness to really share.

I am proud to call Riley my friend and privileged to co-author his debut novel. Riley's personal entries provided more than enough material for the storyline of this fiction work and coupled with my organizational and expository methods; I am highly pleased with our collaboration's product in the form of this book. Now, let's get All Riled Up!

Ted L. Carroll

For Blake Redding.

1 Little Green Army Man

According to state law, even felonies have a five-year statute of limitations. So Rave is safe now. But he'll never act that crazy again. This injury is, for sure, the peak of all the insanity he's yet been through. He says that his crazy days are finally over.

"Time to act my age – and I'm fine with that. I will have a family and a career, hopefully as an innovator – or a writer," says Rave. But, since a career innovating is impractical, for now he is settling to write this book. It's something to do, and finding things to do is difficult, being injured.

❧

Five and a half years ago, Rave met a different kind of girl than he was accustomed to meeting. She took his heart in her hands and shook – and she didn't stop until she got more than she bargained for.

"I have to admit," Rave would blunder, "I got more than I bargained for as well." A child, an ex-lover, a bro' who would do anything for the sake of friendship – and imminent death.

Arguably, though, death is always near. But would such a cocktail take more than Rave had lost already? Fate had him now . . . or purgatory . . . or predestination . . . somehow it was all the same, somehow none of it mattered, nor ever would it, perhaps. Or it mattered more than anything ever would for the remainder of Rave's earthly years.

Annie, this woman who made Rave, by all means, in all ways, like air makes a balloon, like balloons make celebrations – she led him, like a little boy, into worlds he'd only fantasized about – until then.

"Annie," Rave would often say, "What happens when you get bored with me?"

"Oh, you sweet thing," she'd reply with the innocence of a smirking Cheshire, "I love being with you and I love you. I won't get bored with you! Unless you go and die on me. That'd be super boring!"

Her interest was, seemingly, more attached to her phone-in-hand than to her relationship with Rave. But he knew timing was everything with her and, later into the night, once they'd been at the bar for an hour or so, Annie would look into his soul, and he into hers, and even the next morning – for a day or two – even without the drinks, they would lose each other in the depth of one another's eyes – with their hearts and minds – and with their bodies. This took a lot of movement, which Rave would later realize he took for granted more than he, or anyone, could ever really know.

∽∾

On that note, Rave learned that being physically injured is a significant motivator for spirit, mind, and body, too. In fact, Rave has never before so clearly seen the necessity of living for his highest values; and quite honestly, there are many things Rave would like to do before death.

Now, on the other side (so to speak) of a near-death experience, Rave is here with new accessories. Sure, the wheelchair and other par-for-the-course accommodations, but what Rave meant is that he'd been granted insight, awareness, and an uncommon perspective through the doors of heavy drinking, vehicular mishap, a coma, and reawakening.

∂∞∂

The story, in reverse panacea, jig-sawed together in shotgun moments, brief interludes with the Other Side inspiring his active participation in the presence of what could be each and every moment of this life – as Rave had come to find. He records them as he can, only at times – now – and through months of discouragement, excitement, depression, and enlightenment.

Mostly, the story is Rave's; some of it is what could've, should've, would've or, might yet in fact transpire. The rest of the story is another's – one's to do with, "your part," what one will. Rave often invited, "Besides, what do you really want?"

On one such contemplative night around smokes and smokes, he heard, as he often would, the audible resonation of his spirit, in these words:

Cigar gun boxes
Wooden hidden cords
Wall sconces
Like bacon's poop

So, life can seem
On death-and life-beds
Sons and daughter's gleam
So, the story goes

Into nights and into days
Like moving again, Like packing things,
Me, this little green army man.

⌘

Annie promised Rave her hand when he asked for it. Rave describes, "I like to remember that night, in part, different than it actually occurred. Not most of it, just the part where I proposed. I give myself kudos for following through by asking her, so don't get me wrong; but I choked on the ring more than once – and once literally – or, at least, almost.

Just for the record, at one point in the evening (dinner reservations at a new restaurant on the river) I had dropped the ring into a wine glass – because I'd read online that a chardonnay toast was a beautifully traditional, though not outdated, way to propose.

We weren't on a rooftop or the Eifel Tower, hell, not even in Seattle's Space Needle, but a Spokane surf and turf. This was as nearly as nice as formal could get for Spokane, but it was a far cry from the romanticism that dominated my fantasies and pervaded Annie's whims. Truth is, however, she usually settled for the best around, not willing to really search outside her comfort zone, not thus far in her life anyhow.

Annie was just returning from powdering her nose in the steakhouse john just as I'd let loose the princess cut, white gold, 1.5 carat total weight into the bottom of her chardonnay glass top. Unexpectedly, Annie, without sitting down to join me at the river-view's adorned slatted mahogany, grabbed both our glasses! She, then, coupling the glasses together in an impromptu, sloppy embrace, snagged me by the coat and whirled us toward the balcony's patio door. Without the luxury of a moment's pause, she threw a glass into my face and, doing what I always did, I swallowed hard.

She'd offered up the chardonnay preserving my life's promise, which I, unthinkingly, didn't balk at consuming. The lassoed rock caught my tonsil, and, at the last millisecond, I coughed it right into her strawberry blonde, sculpted, salon mess. She didn't have a chance to balk as I grotesquely, unnervingly, apologized (to which she was more than accustomed) as I fingered the ring out of her fruity locks; halfway apathetic to the lost opportunity for life's purpose, I made a slight gesture, to the effect, 'What's true love, anyways, if you can't spit a wad in your girl's hair once a year or so, right babe?'

'Right honey,' Annie whispered back, choked up from the intensity of her nose powder, still. She hadn't heard what I'd said, nor did she know what had landed in her hair as we danced on the patio before the strip and shrimp.

Finally, after replaying all possible scenarios in my head throughout appetizers and the meal, a meek, 'Will you marry me?' squeezed out of my apparently greenish throat–near the downing of her last surf.

'We'd enjoyed a good meal,' I figured, 'We gave our all to the city's view,' I injected into my own evaluative thinking, 'We love Kade' and 'We can build all the life we desire, the three of us.'

So, I proposed – right then and there – even before seeing the dessert cart. I couldn't help but observe the desperately monotonous ordinariness of the circumstantial positioning of The Question – but I was damn proud of myself for finally doing it!

'Kchwahh!' She screeched in a choked cough, out of honest unsuspecting, and then, with inside-duct tears and sincere whimpering, 'Oh yes! Yes, yes, YES!'

I knew everything would be different from that moment. Although, my idea of what 'different' meant then, and what it means today, is a far cry from synonymous."

∾⧟∾

And so Rave and Annie might one day live married. But, until then, they had annals of research to compile. There would be issues, undoubtedly.

∽∞∾

Rave just awoke in the hospital one day, he could barely move – at all. And he couldn't talk. What a trip. Rave did acid once, at the coolest concert hole in Washington, the Gorge at George. The intensity didn't compare – not even near. What did compare was Annie. And his son, Kaden.

Kaden – Kade. He compared. Rave's son was why he lived and wanted the things in life that he wanted. Being a dad, while awesome and wonderful, was unfathomably scary. Understandably, Annie loved Kaden like Rave did – or so he understood her doting's and dreaming's to mean.

While Annie was not Rave's son's biological mother, they both felt that she certainly could be his real mom – at least that is how circumstances were – about three years ago.

∽∞∾

Now, as Rave attempts to remember and record all that has happened since the awakening, waves of terror and some kind of dirty guilt, or maybe shame, surface. Rave is unsure really of what to call it – like seeing a kind of unfamiliar insect for the first time – no frame of reference for description except the abstractions of size and relativities of condition – maybe. He tries recalling every piece of memory and shattered information possible.

Rave feels that remembering everything he can is vital to rehabilitation – in every way – although when asked why this was the case Rave's answer isn't readily grasped. It often seems elusive. The experience is like catching a frog while intoxicated, for sure.

One day, recent, following a physical therapy session, Rave found a summary of his thoughts concerning such banked memories:

Giving (Bank of Memories)

In the end, all there is to take
Are memories, memories, all
That remains in the bank
Of memory…

Make 'm mostly good, I say,
Cuz people die but
Better to die with investments
Than with debits…

So, go – without regret –
Be who you are and
Be the best there's to be.

One day
It ends
All, washed,
Away…

Tabula rasa says
Abandonment results in
Achievement within

Perhaps the best
Of a life – of Life –
To be given, give,
Giving.

2 Getting Wet

Then, it was the best time of his life – or so he thought. More accurately, he expected the enjoyment would continue; still, he's learned that he could be correct about circumstances, the future or, more aptly, the future could be right about him. A strong sense of pleasure prevailed. In fact, Rave was to catch the largest steelhead that he'd ever caught.

"Note to self," Rave heard himself say. "A new spinner is worth the $8.99, every time."

In a way, Rave was very similar, he knew, to the black *Mepps* lure that he'd lost to a crappie while fishing for trout. Long lake, WA, like a country boy's swimmers' hole is to a city lad's jungle gym, so as catching a decent sized trout here is like falling off the old, low, wooden balance beam, rather than the from the rotating, floating, mechanically coasting monkey bars.

Rave recalls texting Annie later that evening*: "I wrote you a story. About fishing on Long Lake. A large Muskie scared the trout that I hooked, right off my line. Then the near-whale came back to my line and swallowed the trout whole, then, my Mepps."*

Rave remembers Annie's reply went something like:
"Chomp that fish! Make it a wedge!"

He didn't know what she meant, really. But her further reply was, *"You're the shit Rave."* Rave knew he loved here, right then. His love was authentic, as material matches socks, and he'd already known of his knocking knees but was scared Annie might not be ready for commitment.

Not that anyone is ready for loving, no one is ever prepared or has what it takes, to simply be there, in love. But knowing this is how some people simply love through life – especially Rave and his kind – the Terminally Unrequited.

∽

So, Rave definitively determined, most probably because of fish and women:

"The love of God is real!" Indeed.

Big fish are brought our way when we get wet and remain to pray!

∽

The fish story reminded Rave of the New Years' Eve girl, the crazy who kissed his best buddy and called it The Mrs. Claus Clause. While Rave let the pseudo-transgression roll off his head, it stuck in his heart like the end of a severed angioplasty tube stuck in the wrong patient's carotid.

"Pseudo nothin'," Rave heard from his (truest) self.

∽

After this dawning, Rave reflected:

"See, there's a kid in me, still. The kid knows what is going on. My adult brain gets in the way a lot – it happens significantly when I think too much. I've observed that, really, almost all adults have lost their sense of what's real. That's one quality, above all, in Kade that I love and admire. And it's him, his essence – and he's here, he exists, because of me – because of my drive, driving into a gorgeous hot bartender; she changed my life – and life changed us, the fire bringing along in the osmosis, Kaden."

Kaden liked dinosaurs. He spent time looking out the window and at animals, including plastic dinosaur figures, in a way that only reminded me of how my knees felt in my stomach when I first touched the bartender.

She, Kade's mom, Zoe, was finding herself – still. That was okay. Rave knew, in truth, that he also, was looking for himself. She was kind enough, at least when she was trying to be nice. He knew, though, that when she wasn't nice her antagonism was due to the fact that she was stressed.

Despite Zoe's angst, Rave saw her in Kade. Their son had her foreface features, Rave's eyes, and Rave's gut – but her lips and cheeks – undeniable. In a seemingly strange light, Rave had to admit that the parts of his face that reflected Zoe somehow helped him to understand her discontentedness.

All mothers, others, and heaviness aside – Annie and Rave were about to embark on the highlight-years of their lives! He was finished fishing. Lures were for fakes. Rave found his. They'd be married.

First, Rave must backtrack, way back.

The furthest time back that Rave could muster a memory, he was at a lake with his family. Rave's mother and father were there, as well as his dog. Rave loved the puppy, Barley. Barley was his best friend – Rave must've been three years old. Or four. Anyhow, the sun was bright, and Rave recalled the breeze on his young unscathed boy-tummy. It was early summer. Rave's dad caught a trout.

"Ravey," Pops said, "Feel its scales."

"Fishy-fishy fish-fish," was all Rave could slip out. A few years after it happened, Rave's father told him that those were his words. Rave kind of doubted him, at the time; those words sounded stupid, he thought. Rave simply knew, however, that he liked being next to Barley – and she liked being next to him.

Today, however, Rave believed his father. He was just a little boy after all and, it wasn't stupid, it was cool – cool to be innocent and free, free to say and be whoever he was.

That simple story made clear what life was meant to be, really.

So, Rave began having fun. And when Rave said fun, he meant that he partied how he hadn't known he was capable of partying previously. Life was a thriller, and he was the soundtrack!

"At last," Rave thought, "I know what it's all about! I know who I am, and I know what to do. Fun makes sense – and I am fun!"

3 Negative Space

Here begins the stories of debauchery and danger. Or, at least, that's how he told it to people then – "back in the day."

✦

"She was whimpering I fucked her so hard. I mean it's one thing when a chick screams, it's a whole other level – when she feels like she's busting in half while you're blaze-canyoning her insides – like her uterus has swallowed her labia minor: petrifying, due to the slaughtering skin-sword that's pillaging her clitropolis."

✦

Rave, in short, was not known for his being couth.

Like a typical beginning of a band session with the dudes, this was just the same. Had more of that experience been true, Rave would never have had to prove his claimed righteousness. He knew that he, hardly ever, actually had to prove myself – but tried anyhow.

Already, at fourteen years of age, Rave was ready for change. Rave's parents had been divorced for a few years and whatever his dad was doing simply sucked, Rave thought. Truth be told, Rave's father was hardcore successful in nearly every way. And the same was true of his mom, although Rave misunderstood her far more than his dad (as he would discover years later). He could justify himself in his mother's eyes more easily than in his dad's – turns out that's a "son-to-mother" thing. Understandable.

Negative space assignment assigned: freshman art class. General. Generally boring. An insane nutjob – or a genuinely kind senior – asked Rave what he thought of God. Rave was not sure about that guy. Turns out he was just a helpful – and genuinely kind – upper classman.

∽∾

Being dependent was the beginning of a new experience for Rave. "It's very annoying," Rave's mother would often hear him say in the several months following the accident, when his formation and expression of words had returned.

From early childhood, Rave was uninterruptedly independent. Sometimes, he was so incredibly set on doing things by himself that his parents feared that he might topple over right into his morning bowl of rice pudding – or the campfire – or whatever happened to be the biscuit du jour.

Rave had such a good-loving heart and he would often hear himself thinking,

"This is so hard, yes so very hard. I am used to helping others with many things. Now, here I am, and I know what I have to do."

Later, Rave would disclose to his mom that, while incomparably difficult, he knew what it was he needed to do; specifically, he went on to explain, paradoxically, that life had suddenly become very, very simple – painfully so.

∽◌◊◌∽

Simplicity always is a determinative solution conjured by the early morning steam of silence rising from putrid pools of complicated maladies.

∽◌◊◌∽

What Rave meant was that he had only one choice now: to accept and to willingly receive help. "I have no choice in the matter," was his daily inner chant. And – his prayer.

In this respect, life became easy. Rave no longer had the variety of common options to alter his frequency. There was now only one station to choose from, but the broadcast was loud and strong; not always pleasant to hear, though the broadcast was nurturing and more than sufficiently comforting.

Later, Rave would recognize the frequency by a specific name, a combination of labels which he came to understand as the loving, unconditional grace of a beautiful, promise-keeping God.

Despite the cheery sound of that perspective, Rave told his father, on more than one occasion,

"I've got nothing to lose. It sounds dangerous – but I am not dangerous. But Dad, I have nothing to lose. I feel trapped, almost. My back is up against a wall, no doubt."

These kinds of statements ate at the heart of Rave's parents who've, only always, wanted him to be happy and fulfilled. They each worried very much about him, at least until he began owning this disclaimer: "I must go up, up is the only way."

Rave's parents as well as many other family members, friends, and acquaintances, saw the lightness of demeanor and hope of life in a renewed way, after witnessing the re-manifesting expressions of Rave's change of heart a few times, continuing.

Rave's friends remember reading this, which Rave had written in the hospital one early morning:

They speak at me
Talking loudly and, oh so slow
Behind this wall, I'm here

Though, they don't know
I want to talk
But silence has me, alone

I close today, a chapter done

Now, I rise unbounded,
Love found me wanting, then
I turned away in utterance,
My own voice – Heaven sent!

Today I stepped!
I! And my brain, did it!
Of course, allowing the help, I need:
I, you, God – We did this!

4 Hummingbird Peacock

Annie and Rave had planned on being married. They often spoke of marriage, especially for the three months following Rave's near-choke of a finely charade proposal.

Something was in the vineyard that season though – like what happens to milk after seventeen hours without power: the tweak of tincture type, twisted-tit tongue turbulent terd trots. Tiny tearing to truest taste. Then – *tata!* Oh, teat.

In other words, the alcohol stopped working quite like it once did. Something had apparently turned sour in the ferment. Time was a partner with the turning. Time always is.

Shortly thereafter, Rave would write:

> I used to swear by something of heaven
> That brought us together
> Like binding to page.
> Then she would swallow and
> I had to follow – and I did,
> But – to my grave.
> I knew she was rotting

From her insides, like sin lies,
As grapefruit to tummy's skin –
Oh! Acid's reply.

∽◦∾

Annie said she wanted this and needed that. Rave delivered, because he could. Sometimes, however, Annie didn't really know what was happening. Rave wasn't sure why she wanted to know, anyway. Annie got whatever she wanted whenever she requested (often demanded) it. She primarily wanted cash and clothes. "Same thing," thought Rave.

Rave never told Annie (of course) but he'd had a crush on her mom, Milly, like he'd only had before on his left hand, in his junior high years. Relentless, overtaking, musty-backpack-crusty-next-day-towel-but-still-damper-moist kind of, perfect slamming boy-love, luster-crush.

"She has me backed into a corner!" Rave thought his heart was telling him.

Oh! Annie's Mom. Milly was killing him. Unknowingly to her – and – to him, but secretly, of course. When Annie and Rave would have sex, Milly's face would enter Rave's psyche-platform; reluctant to leave.

He'd almost cornered Milly on several holiday occasions, but instead had faith in what turned out to be a misplaced door of worship. Despite her seeming evasion, Rave thought, certainly, that she would somehow trap him in the laundry room when he "went downstairs to find the cat." Rave had used that line more than just a couple of times.

He was existentially disappointed that by the third (and even fourth) hint she'd failed to affirm his fantasy.

It's worth mentioning here that, Milly observed Rave like a fluttering little sugar-lusting peacock one mid-afternoon – as he was about to mount her daughter in the family room. Annie didn't see her mom standing nearby, peeking through the room's adjacent doorframe. In fact, in messy distraction, Annie had her head bent down and cocked to the side.

Rave, then, made eye contact with Milly for a decidedly extended time and was deliberate to slightly turn himself (and shift Annie's torso too) so that Milly could see Rave's penis in its full handsome profile thrusting thick full-blood view – as he plunged into Annie as if it was Milly's last day breathing to enjoy such a privileged theatre event.

Milly made no move to look away, rather her eyes were fixated on what must've represented a different time in her private cache of memories.

Several minutes had passed when Rave finally heard footsteps following, in soft dispersion, from Milly's vantage point. She'd loved Rave, more than ever before since that experience. Rave was sure of it; also, a seemingly private jealousy toward her daughter germinated and began growing – to which Rave has yet to see an ending.

But, these days, Milly is one of Rave's greatest caretakers. Her love is pure today; at least, as far as Rave knows. Rave's love for her, while characteristically clean is, in addition, essentially honest.

Annie loved him, then. Or so thought Rave. In the sense of what either one of them knew as love, they loved, and they loved one another ruggedly well. Truth is, the pair may not have known (or been aware of) enough about what loving action means, in practical terms – the commitment and decision that Love asks of each – to follow through with resolutely constructing the idea-towers in which they'd invested and of which they'd dreamt.

Sandcastles, too, like butterfly-wings and puffed hummingbird-bodies, have a unique niche in the order of nature in the universal cosmic unfolding. Rave doesn't regret a day spent with Annie; in fact, as much as he now complains about her, he actually misses her, frequently to the point of despair.

Previous to the discoveries forthwith expressed, Annie and Rave had many an uncommon adventure together.

5 Borealis Foretelling

"They tell me to move and go, to go and move. And all I can do is lay there and move – just enough to urinate – on good days. At least, this is how it was early on in my rehabilitation. Later on, although movement was limited, I began functioning with increased courage and could do more and more on my own. Also, and perhaps more significantly, I imagined life as it could be, in the seemingly distant future. Similarly conveyed, conjuring a vision so apparently fantastical was unimaginably difficult.

While others would continue mostly taking for granted the kinds of victories for which I accrued private accommodative accolades, I certainly knew of only one constant in this tripped-out journey. That one constant would keep me of sound mind: as I maintained listening to what my heart was saying."

. . Thus, Rave continued writing.

❧

Attention led to awareness, awareness to practice, and practice to maintenance.

❧

Months ago, Rave pronounced that he was decidedly finished talking about how awful the injury was, except for some moments of real venting. The truth concerning his current circumstances was that, while everything seemed, at times, worse than ever, all was, in fact, better than it'd ever been. And it was all happening at the same time. The acknowledgement allowed for a sort of lasting experience of transcendence that allowed for continued perseverance and increased means for adaptation. As such, adaptation has led to survival, certain progression, but also to enjoyment.

Now, this quest, intrinsic of all key moments essential to each mirroring stroke of existence, turned its subject toward the Eternal; or perhaps, Eternity turned Rave-ward. However, described, an unveiling was undeniably taking place, like the shroud of Jesus Christ left behind at Golgotha's cave – the sign told not only of one man's miracle – but of the Good News for all humanity.

∝∞∝

One Thursday night Rave and Annie found themselves on Aurora Avenue in Seattle, WA. Months after that dark night, Rave found a napkin with chicken scratch resembling his script; though, due to the nature of Blackout's Well, he may never know its true author:

> Like a partly cloudy day,
> I suppose one could say,
> So is blue and so is gray,
> Partial sunshine, possible rain.
>
> Like respect calls to those who play,
> Life begins one box-top day, there's

Truly not much else to do, but
Pick your sign and roll on through.

At times, dice bounce
Or often turn on a corner, or three,
Like heart, mind, and body –
Respect calls us, as Love does,

To simply be with the ones we love.
The hardest part, perhaps is, with us,
Not for a day or two – but in the one –
Seemingly, so near certain doom.

Yes, the overwhelming sense of 'stay'
Comes in waves, in rolling days –
There comes a promise, along the board,
That asks us to confront our lore –

Like never ever, ever before.
In similar terms, we're asked
To, justly, be the better one
When matched with pain in closest kin.

Now the witness, to death or life,
Is real simplicity – by love or fear –
These very circumstances will
Take us out or keep us near.

≫

Seattle – Aurora – kept us out.

⧉

The night was like halving is to split pea soup: definitive. Leather bars and techno clubs taught the couple lessons of places they didn't really want to go (except so badly) and an introduction to volumes of chapters they'd promised themselves they'd never entertain – but had fantasized about and proceeded to repeat, unhesitatingly, throughout most of their time's embrace.

Unfortunate, some may say, but the Dragon of Hell impregnated Annie that night. The dragon's name?.. Brown.

Heroin effortlessly took its toll – as the entire bridge and its passerby – and without regard for any discrimination. None whatsoever. She may not admit such possession, still today, but the haze of subtle Satanism was upon her like fog on an inlet – suspecting but frozen. She used foil like animals would – and robbed herself, not just of future husbandly orgasms, but of sweetest-type serotonin spikes that are (or in her case, would've been) natural to stocking stuffed Christmas mornings; instead (and sometimes of grace alone) she merely feigned copied smiles, stenciled from the faces of non-demon-attended relatives.

"Annie, Annie," Rave repeated, again and again, "Can you hear me? Annie. Annie!"

Annie didn't respond. She couldn't. Rave hadn't yet been convinced of her incapacitation, despite the onset of grayish blue lips and fingertips; his own haze kept him from acknowledging truth – it was that simple.

"She's fine," Rave heard himself say, without words, "She must be fine, she looks like herself still." Although, at the time, Rave didn't understand his own thinking, he knew later that he nearly let his fiancée die; in fact, if Rave's best friend,

Brode, hadn't walked behind the bar three minutes into Rave's apparent time lapse, Annie wouldn't have survived.

"Rave! What the fuck are you doing? She's probably dead already, dude!" Still, Brode's presence – though whiskey buzzed – was certainly coherent and lively, but it didn't snap Rave back to the consciousness of what was actually happening in the moment. Annie was very near death. Brode could've gone either way with the drugs Annie still had concealed under her jacket.

Of all people who knew where Annie kept her stash, besides Rave, Brode did. See, Brode and Annie had danced with the dragon as a threesome at another period in the friends' brief lives. Rave, thinking later, wondered – thankfully – at why Brode hadn't used Annie's "left over" smack on himself. Brode, reservedly, was able to stick with just booze. The bottle, for Brode, still worked fine – and good enough for him.

"Annie's here, Annie's here," was all that Rave could muster toward Brode.

"Yah, no shit dipfuck!" Brode snagged off in Rave's direction, while simultaneously pulling out his mobile phone, dialing 9-1-1 and, ultimately, saving Annie's life.

While Rave was in a daze, the paramedics arrived who secured Annie on a stretcher after slamming her with Nar-can and shoveling her into the ambulance. She's alive today thanks to Brode. Upon awakening, Rave felt – in his words – "Like a piece of shit."

Rave recovered from his feeling of remorse quickly. By five o'clock that evening – his first drink of the day.

6 Lucky Camper

Kaden awoke next to his papa that morning. He looked at Rave in the eyes, after crawling up on his chest to get the very best view of his daddy's eyes. The love shared between Rave and Kade was the purest kind of love that exists. Love like that needed nothing for itself. Presence was enough, just existing, nurtured more from their impenetrable bond than most humans ever have the pleasure to know.

"Dad!"

"What buddy?"

I want Lucky Charms.

"Yep."

"Get me them."

"Okay."

"Thanks Dad."

Kade went to the couch while Rave went into the kitchen for the bowl of cereal and milk. He brought it to his boy, who had already distracted himself with his papa's tablet. He sat on the brown suede sofa, watching cartoons when Rave delivered the meal.

"I love you Kade."

"I love you too Dad."

Kade would remember these mornings with his dad and, Rave with his son, for the rest of their natural lives. Kade, in the always-not-too-far-away-days, would tell his new school friends, "My dad's the coolest." Rave would smile, often sitting at home, knowing, one: he created life, two: life is good, and three: he somehow heard the boy say these things – but without really having heard. He didn't need to hear, in Time. Time was only a method. Fathers who've known a certain fear understand this kind of connection. Joy and peace are its flipsides.

Being a father is magical – or it's not. As love always does, fatherhood presents choice like a weekend's heavy snow brings silence. Nothing can be asked, or taken, from reality. So, love, like water, still, flows.

Rave caught himself secretly plotting events that would forever alter the lives of his lovers. Zoe was at the top of that list. He caught himself fantasizing about the prospect of hacking into Zoe's financial records and creating havoc, just because he was resentful.

Soon, Zoe was forever lost to a life of shallow enterprise. Rave would forget about her altogether – except for one day a year – Kade's birthday. She never sent a card – or anything. Rave, on this single day only, rented her a limited, very small, space in his mind – for the sake of his love for Kade. No other reason he thought was sufficient save this one.

Rave, soon after the Aurora fizzle, grew weary of Annie's escapades-delirium. He began to turn inward to his deepest self. Next thing he knew, Rave was at his go-to watering hole – and reefed out of his skull. He began pounding shots with nothing but a good time in mind.

Shot after jacked shot, Rave began having visions of rainbow eucalyptus trees, as he would describe the particularity of this event months later. Awakenings are like this: transformative and fantastical, like when grandpas give grandkids yoyos like foil-wrapped Big Red cinnamon-gum sticks.

Rave began hearing and seeing like he hadn't ever been able to before. He began to write. He wrote – as if he'd always been writing. He loved to create. In the spirit of such creation, thinking of how he might reconnect with Annie – contemplating the choice of hateful or neutral deeds toward Zoe, hard-petting himself while looking at old Facebook photos of Milly, revisiting the birth of Kaden, remembering the appearance of former friendships (especially with Brode) prior to a typical night's unfamiliarly familiar shots of Jack – contemplating these recollections, Rave wrote:

"Relationships, of all kinds, are both love and hate. Imagine a dial with a mechanical needle pointed up from the bottom center. Does it lean more toward Love or Hate? Which reading is on the left and which on the right? What scales are in between? Perhaps it gives an accurate reading of your character. Being centered, allowing the needle to be centered, is Ideal. One needs both good and bad. One doesn't exist without the other. Being best means a balance of both."

Rave, after the next day or so of pleasurable self-pity, recalled a trip he took to North Idaho. Although the excursion was just a few months back, many of the details had been blacked out for much of the time, from Rave's return home from that trip until a very recent time. Rave was reminded, mostly, by the "failure to appear" and thus a bench warrant notification he retrieved from the mailbox one day not long ago.

In fact, touching the officially textured manila envelope triggered the sensory recall of cutting lines of cocaine on Brode's open tailgate, amongst other places around the campsite. Next, Rave, Brode, Annie, and Jimmy (a new, incidental-to-the-trip, acquaintance) unloaded Jimmy's CR 500 – which toted the quickest displacement capability in circuit. So, Rave, like his liquid alcohol, preferred the earth shattering and most effective recreation vehicle. What happened though, with bikes and straws, was more than he bargained for – at least three times out of ten.

The dilemma of speed and, well, speed – although it would've provided a phenomenal batting average, the percentage was truly an inclination pointing toward embarrassment and disaster – it occurred all too frequently for the comfort of Rave and his companions.

The same was true for the nearby party, to whom Rave, and his troupe was camping. In fact, when the gray haired, flannel sporting neighbor lady awoke and sat down (in the hazy-dim dusk of dawn, yet without the coffee's campfire started) she was disgusted to find the wild group's gift of the nighttime: a not-so-delicate package of previously undisturbed feces; at this point in her morning, however, the lady screamed in horror and then, "damn those 'coons!" In extra-heavy, blow-fueled, Everclear-drenched, blacked-out debauch – Rave or one of his mates, had crapped on the grunge-woman's favorite chair.

"That must have been a big 'coon!" Rave and his buddies heard this exclaimed by the poor woman that morning. The group of friends rolled in laughter over that one, then, and still today. Undoubtedly.

Besides all that excitement, "the most amazing bike ever" was lodged under a half-tree in a lake-sized mud puddle. The contraption was steaming for the remainder of that fruitless night and into the following day. Rave, upon seeing the messed-up machine, immediately keeled over from acute pain in his ankle; he looked down to see a gnarled mangle of inextricable foot and sock material – and blood – dried but shiny.

Consequently, Rave would carry a felony warrant for that weekend, due to driving recklessly and evading authorities at a roadblock. Needless to say, the remainder of the outing mirrored the adventure's first few events: hard to recall and surely regrettable. No one died but fun was had. So – "Another successful trip," as defined by its attendees.

Oh – Except that hippie-logger camper-neighbor lady.

Friggin' party pooper.

7   Jacked Holy Roller

Annie, after a sober hiatus of approximately four months, called Rave. It was Sunday. She suggested, "Especially since it'd been a while," that she and Rave get together to "hang out." Rave, thrilled but surprised to hear from her, was horny and thought meeting Annie – anywhere for any reason – especially if it involved potential intoxication (and penetration) was, indeed, a definitively grand proposal.

Predictably, within an hour, the two met behind a nearby bar. Annie embraced Rave, pretending anger, thrusting him by his shoulders into the still-opened door of her teal Durango, ripping down his jeans, briefs, and initiating a years' personalized fellatio, which he'd been missing for months, until now.

When Annie had finished draining Rave's extremities, the pair – then hiking up his hitchers together – switched positions, as he took his turn releasing the trapped spirits of her netherworld. Next, the couple pranced across the asphalt parking lot into the barroom, like kids from the schoolhouse to the playground: free and unsuspecting.

Annie, without Rave having a clue, slipped some liquid methadone in his first shot of Jack after heading into the girls' room to shoot heroin between her legs. Her thigh, nearest the pelvic bone, around the side but before the flank, offered her the carotid, the quickest route home. Rave, "done" after his first holy roller, ordered a bottle anyway, proceeding to pound shot after shot.

He also ordered (and rapidly devoured) some nacho fries and garlic chicken wings. In fact, although no one but Rave remembers this now, he apparently choked on a chicken bone in the midst of his blacking out, but luckily a pepper-sizzling university nursing student (or so Rave recalls) grabbed him from behind and Heimlich' d him – indeed saving him from choking to death on the hollowed bit of fowl carcass.

Rave soon left the bar without Annie, who had promptly nodded off in the stall -upon her continued intravenous enlightenment – climbing into his mid-90s, cream-white, board-paneled Jeep Wrangler – and proceeded to turn the ignition.

Rave jumped into the classic four-wheel drive and slowly rolled out of the parking lot. From the bar, as the back tires rolled off the final edge of the driveway ramp, Rave felt (quite unsuspecting) a sense of power in him that was hitherto unexplainable.

He was not thinking of his newfound laser sense of cosmic infallibility – he simply sped down the road, wet from the days' consistent drizzle, not much faster than he usually drove. Rave, not thinking about much at all, ran over a small bump in the road, overcorrected, incidentally jumping a curb, and barreling across the lawn of an unsuspecting residence, smashing driver's side first into a large pine tree.

Silence.

Emptiness.

Rave awoke. He couldn't move. He couldn't talk. Awake – but still awakening – and in slow motion. Something in his brain turned on fast, but everything else was slowed, slowed down like when a fifty-cent machine wind-up toy penguin loses its speed after beginning its initially speedy waddle. The quickness of a wind-up waddling penguin loses its motivation rather quickly – in the last –*dle* of its final wad-*dle*, so his soul was just like that in a parallel second; his brain, ironically, raced.

Rave's body, a whole separate thing, proved its case far more differently than even the soul or the mind. His body, hardly present, was occupied in anchoring a new experience, like a foreign ship paradoxically in a familiar harbor. Rave was the mast but without sail, just a lonely metal rudder and shell, intently attempting a new kind of (seemingly directionless) guiding.

Rave, shortly after the wreck, as soon as linear thinking returned to him, recalled the words he then wrote:

When I wake up, I feel healed
Then realize I'm injured as
Agony sets its teeth
Securing reality's investment into me.

Like the absolution of drug withdrawing This worst overage hangs me out to dry, Called: Stupid Awakening – Night after night and every day –

Hope has outlasted me,
So, people say, but I know – I know,
Injured or not – or not,
Life's hard either way.

There's not much more to say about what had happened. Summarily, Rave drank at a bar with his girl and lost control of perception in the flash of just another similar second – and crashed. His brain injury, like all too many in such instances, was termed "traumatic," at which he balked for years with a firm "no shit" to anyone who inclined an ear. There were many. Rave, though, was listening for the one ear that mattered most, which was his very own elusive attention-piece. But he continued, instead, to seek the ear of Annie.

Annie was the love of Rave's life. There was not much room for compromise. And certainly, no space remained for Rave's ego, except to lay in her. And so, he did.

Through months of intellectual re-stimulation practices and physical therapy sessions, as well as intent shouting matches with God and with his soul's soul, Rave pushed through, or rather – was pushed through – to another time and place. Soon, Rave was walking.

Albeit a slow process, Rave would walk laps around the nearby Target store for practice in relearning the strides of perseverance. "Ambulatory procedure" took on a novel and purposeful meaning for Rave. His friends and family cheered him on. Rave, while thankful for the moral and practical support, appreciated the actions of trust – especially from Kade, from Annie – and, that which he valued the very most, respect from his dad.

❦

Perhaps, most pointedly, through all of the effort in healing was Rave's utter abandonment of his life to God. While certain people couldn't (or simply wouldn't) understand, Rave saw the fruits of his faith unmistakably clear. Anyone with courage enough to stick by Rave's side, even for a moment, witnessed the subtle but concise effects that prayer and faith had on Rave's physical, mental, and spiritual condition – a seemingly painstaking journey, but with an essentially transformative result.

On the best days, the buoyancy of Rave's spirit shined true, brightly reflecting his profession in the saving grace and restorative nature of being in relationship with Jesus Christ: mustard seeds proved to transplant mountains, the winds of song leveled daily hills, and whatever was requested – that aligned with the goodness of true Abundance – was provided.

༄

Often, only Rave and God knew that which had transpired. Long roads of rebuilding usually require a community – though such infrastructure grows seasoned in an isolation not chosen. That was Rave's experience, most certain.

༄

Rave would go on to speak in front of schools, hospitals, rehabilitation institutions, as well as youth-focused drug and alcohol treatment centers. He'd, on many of these occasions read a poem he'd written, and found post-event, with his belongings:

I have the best of care,
Family and friends here,
Allowing me to be me
Not judging, staying nearby.

Even if I could speak,
I wouldn't know what to say,
These people sticking by me
Each step of the way.

Often, I wonder,
What is it for everyone?
Keeping him or her so close,
Loving – despite my condition.

8 Annie Onward

Annie had to go out and lose herself several more times – until she realized it was when she stopped looking that she was truly found – and found again and again – or so it seemed to her. On that note, every time she went looking for "true love," an inward sense of painful insatiability always drew her back to Rave.

On the road back to Rave, one day Annie thought it would be a good idea to take Kade on an outing to the local zoo. Kade was five years old and now growing even more thrilled with dinosaurs. Annie thought it would be fun to show Kade the snake-lair exhibit, "Kind of like the babies of dinosaurs," she'd described reptiles to Kade on one occasion.

Annie didn't tell Rave of her plan this time, because almost every other Saturday afternoon she'd take Kade to the ice cream parlor – to give Rave a break from his weekend fathering routine. After all, Kade was created from an unyielding energetic obdurateness, familiar – like oxygen – to generations of *annies* and *raves*.

Thus Rave, thinking Annie was taking Kade for ice cream, didn't ask any questions. She was supportive and Rave was willing to trust her – still – even after everything. Countless times, Annie and Rave severed the bonds of trust in setting the stage for their dance, the choreography of which always brought them, necessarily, to the intense precipice of their next move.

❧

This time was not different; it was a certain overcasting of a time not far in the future – if they would be alive together in the same room again was yet to be determined. Rave said goodbye to his son that day with the nonchalance of merely stepping outside to get the mail.

Kade then waved a sincere "Bye Dada," as Annie, shrugging, promised to return the child within four hours' passing.

Kaden was wearing a shirt sporting "Be good…" on the front and "…You can fall back in it" on its back. Rave began selling tee shirt logos via social networking and sales websites on an ask-and-buy-on-demand basis. This particular shirt was produced fast, distributed quickly, and sold well. Rave received complimentary children's shirts for all his designs. The one Kade wore to the zoo that day was one of the freebie samplers.

❧

Annie omitted telling Rave that her former heroin dealer's younger brother, an acquaintance of Brode, was recently hired at the ice cream spot. While being the younger brother of a dealer, Annie was not hesitant to ask her connection to serve her more than a cold treat; in fact, she asked for a sixteen ounce "cool cup" to go, in paper a bag. Annie had promised herself, Rave, and everyone else in her life, that she was "done"– that the dragon was not only at bay "this time" but that, veritably, the monster was finally slain. So, treats after all, despite the zoo plans.

Kade, though quiet and naturally innocent, knew what his ward was scheming, before anyone else. Indeed, Kade's intuition had caused his fresh young heart to become so aligned with the truth that – by the time Annie had purchased his Bubble Gum Blaster and resorted to the kind of blinding that only an overvalued under-weighed bag of brown can accomplish to otherwise human eyes – he'd grabbed her phone as she prepared rigs for loading.

Kade silently wondered how stupid she must've thought he was, to be engaged in the apparent suicide right in front of his face. "What, just because I am entirely stoked about my Bubble Gum Blaster, she thinks I am totally unaware?" The thought made the little five-year-old fume. He trusted his Uncle Brode, so Kade texted him, saying, "SHE IS DOING IT AGAIN ICE CREAM PLACE THIS IS KADE BIGGER BAG CRAAZY."

Brode, without thinking twice, feeling the dimming lights of Aurora surrounding again, jumped in his car, and shot cautiously for the parlor. Annie was crying now. Kade was slurping his Blaster, faster and faster – a subconscious attempt at avoidance or order– depending on the moment. Rave, blissfully unknowing, at home, felt a slug in his stomach and noticed his throat tighten. He considered it an uncommon digestive response to his routine pizza order, but shrugged it off, unthinking.

Annie, whatever was going through her head, injected the first rig with such unmatched delight that she uncontrollably snatched another (of four rigs cocked and ready) fingering it like a cigarette while, fumbling, she lit a menthol blend and reversed quickly out of the parking lot – unconsciously intent on showing Kaden the snakes. Kade froze with fear. Her driving was not alarming, but premonitions of what could happen rushed over him like colder water seems in a rainstorm to river rocks.

Relentless.
Unpredictable.
Calculating.

The thought came to Annie's awareness, something Rave had shared with her when on a good date (such times were few and far between but nonetheless true despite the infrequency).

Annie, in a state of near-orgasm, "heard" the colors orange and purple, and "saw" the musical score of the Suzanne Vega song, Tom's Diner – as if yesterday was a dinner guest, who showed up for brunch instead, and on a day differing from what a lonely hall's calendar showed in print. Yellowed walls and eggshell paints seemed to creep inside her with each drag of her smoke; simultaneously, Annie read Rave's words from the atmosphere as if she was cloaking herself with each character, like endless warm sleeves of a goose-down quilted layer – and she saw, scribed across a green sky:

"You have to have the right balance of pride. You can have too much pride in one thing while not possessing enough in another. That kind of balance, in regard to pride, is necessary in all areas of life. For example, in sports, one may express skillful application and perhaps exceed all others in result; but there's no perfection had, by anyone, for the entire duration of the activity over time.

Accuracy says there's always more to the show than putting on a performance.

Accuracy says the show itself is a composition; components are individual, as moves in physicality, and must form a fluidity, or die. So, making correct decisions always is always going to manifest as challenge. For instance, 'Do I kick the ball to the right or to the left of the goalie?' 'Do I swing high or low at the baseball?' So, if you're cooking dinner, and what you've created you know is good, be proud. Displaying pride is one's obligation to the rest of us.

Let's say critics and those experiencing fits of jealousy pick the dinner apart. There's no problem but theirs; for him or her, theirs is a problem of non-acceptance. People can be polite and express delight, no matter an outcome. The response, versus a reaction, is an issue of perception. Pay the chef compliment not based on flavor but centered in respect of the creative process. The cook created, shared – not you."

Annie's head bounced on her shoulders like a badly damaged bobble-head. The effects of heroin are relentless, like an Alaskan avalanche in springtime.

Humbly unstoppable.
All consuming.
Unasked for.

༺◈༻

Unsure of anything in her state of mind (or rather her departure from mind) Annie hazily acknowledged the insanity of her thoughts' timing, begging relevance.

Brode intuitively followed Annie's scent; in his conscious mind he heard, "Let the bitch die – 'gotta get Kaden, gotta save Kade." He wouldn't, not for decades anyhow, realize that anything else was happening in the moment.

Above all, Brode was a good friend. He was loyal, but his loyalty was conditional.

The right circumstances filtered in and out of Rave's and his friendship since kindergarten. They were like little schoolgirls on some level and like military brothers on another. Truth be told, their brotherly intimacy was threatening to each in his own way – but it kept them close even when they weren't near – in body, mind, and in spirit too. Only genuine best friends know that strength of bond.

Brode sensed Kade's presence and followed the hidden director. He pulled up from the south to Annie's north-facing car. He stopped not short but rather pulled up as near as metals and paints can be without scraping.

Kade breathed in some bubble gum relief; this time wasn't the first that Brode had saved his life – or so he felt.

Rave, still at home, had drifted into a deep REM sleep; his dream in that few moments was an intense metaphorical vision of life in Hell: rodents, coldness, darkness, and a grinding of bones – blood – and an everlasting, unquenchable sadness that represented the hellishness of death, like the worst of even Life's births.

Annie, during the transcendental hearing, had poked herself once more, leaving three full rigs on the seat next to her. She'd parked the car in a remote parking lot, near pine trees and foliage that, mostly, shielded her vehicle from the main road. The second full rig's content seeped into her bloodstream quickly. Brode knew, without knowing, what was happening.

Through the bullhorn-raw energy of his and Rave's friendship, Brode felt Kade's heart reflecting that of Annie's and, while the child was being rescued from physical danger due to Annie's successful (albeit unaware) securing of the car, Kade's pervasive loving spirit shuddered with the presence of demonic forces – which were attempting to steal the remaining tones from Annie's sweet instrument.

As a couple more years passed most everyone, who knew Rave at one time or another, forgot that he had ever crashed a car into a time entitled "Traumatic Brain Injury." Unsuspecting, so time's road often turns, Rave now walked often and his voice, as reflected in his expressed truth, was clearer than it had ever been – at least ever since he'd uttered his first "dada."

❧

Rave grew into time like time grows into a pumpkin patch. First slowly, then green, next yellow, and orange, and finally against autumn skies, a spectrum encompassing the Unspeakable.

❧

Milly, through all the drama of offspring, stood tall and mysteriously sexy against the backdrop of uncertain times. Like winter, she was respected, sometimes out of necessity only. Annie survived the trials of her past. She would go on to finally wed Rave and act as mother to Kade. Brode served as "uncle," and made a damn fine relative and friend to both Kade and, still, to Rave.

Rave, likewise, was adopted by Brode and Brode's young family, naturally gaining uncle-hood of his buddy's children – like Brode always had for Kade. Annie outlasted her incidentally suicidal tendencies and fatalistic drug addiction, following Rave to a path of Christian living.

Rave, while constantly making strides for himself and his sphere of influence, served his family, friends, and community well, achieving keynote speaker status at regional universities – not to mention the number of individual lives he affected by simply telling his story of wreckage, restoration, and rebirth.

Kade grew into his life, as do most young kids, with unquestioning optimism and seeking of affirmation in unique skills. Primarily, Kade was a happy pony-league football star, achieving elementary headlines, declaring his dad not only his favorite fan but also his best example of inspiration and dreams fulfilled.

ABOUT THE AUTHORS

J. Riley Higginbotham

Riley, a longtime resident of Spokane, WA, born in Tokyo, Japan, has also resided in Seattle and in San Francisco (including, 1234 Haight Street, the renowned complement to Ashbury Street, the intersecting birthplace of, amongst other events, the anti-war hippie awakening and America's mindfulness movement).

Being interviewed for this book, Riley said, "I'm a straightforward guy. I don't like too much talk. But I think honesty is always best. It's better to face your problems head on. Procrastination will drag you down every time. So will beer and girls, especially when mixed."

All Riled Up is Riley's first published book.

Ted L. Carroll

Co-authoring All Riled Up, Ted compiled and edited Riley's personal notes, reformatting and incorporating the entries into a fiction story that, to a believable extent, parallel Riley's coming-of-age wreckage and his renewed spiritual initiation.

Carroll, a Spokane author and social services professional whose current focuses are Behavioral Analysis, and Marriage and Family Therapy, is the author of Amazon-ranked The Weathering of Strawberry Ben, The Strawberry Ben Spiritual Workbook: Co-Creating Everyday Eternal Living, and Illegal Jesus: Young Immigrant Hispanic Males in Strata-Fractured America – An Invitation to Americans from Within.

Further, Ted is a devoted family man. A faithful and devout follower of Jesus Christ, Ted maintains enhancive complementary practices (in addition to Christian perspectives of all denominations and traditions) from significant Buddhist, Native American, Muslim, Jewish, Hindi, and Sufi influences (among others). Eclecticism, with a heart for Jesus, lights Ted's path.

All Riled Up is Ted's fourth published work.

CONTACT THE AUTHORS

Please visit As You Are Publishing's Website for the most recent book release information and news:

www.asyouarepublishing.wix.com/buythebook

Also, please contact Riley or Ted directly: rileyhigginbotham@ yahoo.com tedcarrollauthor@outlook.com

www.tedcarrollauthor.wix.com/buythebook

Thank you for reading. If you enjoyed the experience, please take a moment, and submit a review at your preferred online retailer.

Thank you, Riley & Ted